Williamson W Publishing

Make Your Own

CHRISTMAS ORNAMENTS

Ginger Johnson

Illustrations by
Norma Jean Martin-Jourdenais

Quick Starts for Kids!®

Williamson Publishing Charlotte, Vermont

Library of Congress Cataloging-in-Publication Data

Johnson, Ginger, 1946-
    Make your own Christmas ornaments / Ginger Johnson ; illustrations by Norma Jean Martin-Jourdenais.
        p. cm. -- (Quick starts for kids!)
    ISBN 1-885593-79-1
    1.   Christmas tree ornaments--Juvenile literature. 2. Handicraft--Juvenile literature. I. Title. II. Series.
    TT900.C4 J62 2002
    745.594' 12--dc21

                                                    2002009424

Quick Starts for Kids! ® series editor: **Susan Williamson**
Interior design: **Dana Pierson**
Interior illustrations: **Norma Jean Martin-Jourdenais**
Cover design: **Marie Ferrante-Doyle**
Cover photographs: **Peter J. Coleman**
Cover illustrations: **Michael Kline**
Printing: **Quebecor World**

Williamson Publishing Co.
P.O. Box 185
Charlotte, VT 05445
(800) 234-8791

Manufactured in Canada

10 9 8 7 6 5 4 3 2

Dedication

To Eric

Acknowledgments

Special thanks to friends who shared their favorite ornaments with me. Thanks to Susan Williamson of Williamson Publishing, who inspired me to stretch my talents as a writer and craftsperson. Without the support, friendship, and laughter of my editors, Vicky Congdon and Emily Stetson, this book would not have been finished on time! To Dana Pierson for design and to Jean Silveira for proofing, I am grateful. A thank-you to Norma Jean Martin-Jourdenais for producing detailed and exact illustrations. They're perfect! Lastly, hugs to my husband, who put up with messy craft projects and late nights on the computer, and provided the encouragement for me to publish.

Contents

Christmas Ornaments...
from me to you!

Making Christmas ornaments was always a tradition for my family when I was growing up. We would begin months before we ever had "visions of sugarplums" dancing in our heads. (In fact, we often got started on those hot days of summer, when working quietly was the only way to stay cool.) Craft time would begin by gathering ribbons, clothespins, pom-poms, sequins, and felt. After sharing ideas and deciding on various projects, the fun would begin! I can almost smell the tree and taste the hot cocoa (or lemonade if it was summer). If I close my eyes, I can still picture my room gradually filling up with my handmade crafts, just waiting to be hung or placed on gifts. What pleasure! What fun!

Now, I hope that you, too, will enjoy ornament-making, whether it is a quiet time by yourself, a time just for you and a buddy, or a noisy time to be shared by family and friends around a big table. If you begin early enough, your tree could have 25 new ornaments by Christmas! Many of these ornaments may be adapted for uses throughout the year, too. (Valentine woven hearts are a must!) Why not surprise someone with the St. Nick ornament that can be mailed in an envelope, just like a Christmas card? Now that would be fun to give *and* to receive!

So, dream a bit! Start a wonderful tradition! Select your first ornament, gather the supplies, and have fun in the process of creating. You can make these any time of year wherever you live. I hope making ornaments will become a special tradition for you, too!

Ginger Johnson

Basic Ornament-Making Supplies

Check the specific materials needed for the ornament you want to make, then scrounge around a bit before you begin. Chances are, you already have most of what you need right at home.

Pattern-making supplies

cereal-box cardboard
craft scissors
pencil
ruler
tracing paper

Miscellaneous craft supplies

acrylic paints & paintbrushes
batting or cotton balls
beads
craft foam sheets
craft scissors (for paper
    and other materials)
craft wire or floral wire
decorative papers
embroidery floss
fabric or felt
fabric scissors (for fabric
    only)
feathers
glitter

glue
markers
needle-nose pliers (for work-
    ing with wire)
pom-poms
raffia
ribbon
sequins
sewing needles & thread
shells
Styrofoam balls
tape
toothpick or nail
yarn

Quick Starts Tips!™

Start a craft box for year-round fun! If crafting is your thing or if you'd like to be able to work on ornaments any time of year, then a craft box is a great way to simplify your life. In the mood to craft? Just pull out the box (or maybe two) that contains all of the things you have collected or need. I like to keep two boxes: one for my collectibles, scraps, and trims and the other for tools like craft scissors, fabric scissors, a glue gun and glue sticks, tracing paper, pencils, and markers, plus all my ornament patterns stored in a plastic bag (page 37). My collectibles box is brimful of pieces of ribbon, yarn, fabric and felt scraps, plus shells, sea glass, glitter, pieces of old costume jewelry to take apart (with permission), beads, and buttons. What's going to be in your craft boxes?

MERRY CHRISTMAS ORNAMENTS

Spinning Bead Spiral

Make a light-catching spiral of beads that twists and spins on its own! I make mine with an assortment of round accent and seed beads in different sizes and colors, plus slender tube-shaped bugle beads. For even more pizzazz, add gold balls or pearl beads, or mix emerald green beads to make a sparkling "evergreen" spiral.

❄ Materials ❄

Needle-nose pliers
Beading wire, 20" (50 cm)
Beads, assorted colors and
    sizes
Ruler
Gold thread, 10" (25 cm),
    for hanging

To string the beads

1. Use the pliers to make a small loop in one end of the wire.

2. Begin by sliding a large bead onto the wire until it rests against the end loop. Continue to add beads to complete your first pattern (see *Quick Starts Tips!*™, page 7). Then, repeat the pattern until you've covered most of the wire.

3. Trim the wire with the pliers just beyond the last bead, leaving about ½" (1 cm). Make a small ending loop.

REPEAT THIS PATTERN 10 TIMES
TO COMPLETE THE DESIGN

To form the spiral

1. Beginning at the top, bend the wire into a small circle. Continue to bend the wire around this first circle, creating a spiral of about four circles.

2. Bend the top bead up to form a point. Attach the gold thread through the wire loop; knot the ends. Adjust the spiral as you hold the ornament, pulling on the bottom bead to separate the circles, making your ornament longer, as desired.

3. Hang the beaded spiral where it has plenty of room to spin!

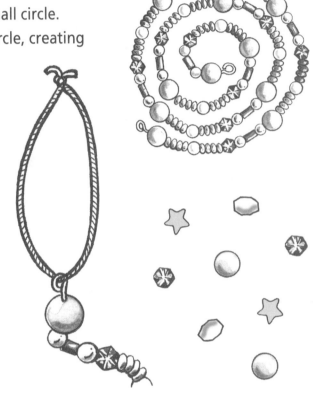

Quick Starts Tips!™

Plan your bead pattern. A design that repeats about every 1½" (4 cm), repeating about 10 times along the length of wire, makes for a really nice balanced spiral. For best results, keep the color pattern to three main colors. My favorite is a mix of metallic-looking green, purple, and bronze beads, with accent and spacer beads of gold and pearl white, but a spiral of clear glass beads and spacer beads picks up all the colors of the Christmas lights.

Miniature Felt Mittens

I like to use felt for this super-simple ornament because then the edges don't unravel when cut. And felt comes in *sooo* many bright colors! The ribbon between the mittens makes the hanger for your tree!

❄ Materials ❄

Template supplies: tracing paper, craft scissors, cereal-box cardboard

Felt: 6" x 6" (15 x 15 cm) square of white or other color, plus scraps of red and green for decorating

Pen, for tracing onto felt

Straight pins

Fabric scissors

Glue gun or craft glue

Batting scraps or cotton balls, for stuffing

Ribbon, 18" (45 cm), for hanging

To make the mitten

1. Trace the two MITTEN templates (page 58) onto tracing paper and cut out. Trace the templates onto cardboard, label, and cut out.

2. Fold the felt in half. Trace the cardboard mitten pattern onto the felt; then, move the pattern and trace again.

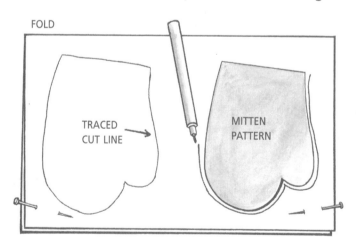

FOLD

TRACED CUT LINE →

MITTEN PATTERN

3. Pin the two felt layers to hold them in place. Use fabric scissors to cut out the mittens, cutting through both layers so that you end up with four felt mitten shapes.

4. Pin two felt mittens together. Glue mitten pieces together around the edges with a bead of continuous glue, leaving an opening at the straight edge. Let dry.

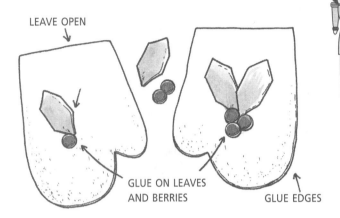

LEAVE OPEN

GLUE ON LEAVES AND BERRIES

GLUE EDGES

5. Lay out the mittens thumb to thumb. Glue on holly. Cut berries out of scraps of felt and glue on.

Quick Starts Tips!™

- **Try other sizes.** Make mitten patterns in different sizes, for a whole family of mittens for your tree. Label each one with the name of someone in your family.

- **Try other shapes.** Horse around a bit! Use a felt horse shape to make a CHRISTMAS HOBBY HORSE (page 32) ornament that doubles as a candy cane holder!

6. Lightly stuff each mitten with batting or a cotton ball. Glue the wrist closed. Let dry. Tie small bows at both ends of the ribbon. Glue one bow to the wrist of each mitten. Let dry.

More Quick Starts Fun!

Make a mitten-ornament tree to raise money for charity! To make a mitten tree, ask a group of friends to help make mitten ornaments. Use all different colors so your tree will be brightly colored. Ask a local store or your school principal if you can put an artificial Christmas tree up and decorate it with mittens. Then, everyone who donates one dollar (use the honor system) can take one pair of mittens.

You can raise money — as much as $100 if you're ambitious — to give to a charity for the needy. Congratulations! You really know the spirit of Christmas!

Hanging Seed Mosaic

Have a ball making this mosaic egg — from plain old seeds! It works well with birdseed, dried peas and beans, and pumpkin or squash seeds — even popcorn. (It's also a great way to use up leftover garden seeds, but ask before using up the garden stash.) Pick an assortment of seed colors and sizes, and then let your creativity go wild. The "seeding" design is best done over several sittings, so be patient!

❄ Materials ❄

Egg-shaped Styrofoam ball
Craft glue
Paintbrush
Tissue paper, tan or another neutral color
Pencil
Seeds in different sizes and colors: sunflower,
    popcorn, radish, squash, lentils, bean,
    split peas, birdseed
Raffia, 12" (30 cm), for hanging
Ruler
Urethane varnish, semi-gloss (optional)

To make the mosaic ornament

1. Coat a section of the Styrofoam ball with glue. Tear off a small section of tissue paper, place over the glue, and brush the edges with more glue. Continue to cover the ball a section at a time until the ball is covered in tissue. Let dry completely.

Quick Starts Tips!™

Seed shortcuts. Make your medallion (page 11) out of *large* seeds. That way you will be finished faster. Or, put a colorful seed pattern on part of the papered egg and leave the rest without seeds. It still looks great and takes much less time and patience.

2. Sketch the design for your *medallion* — a large circular section — on the front of the egg. Then, starting at the center and working out, cover a section with glue. Create the medallion design in the center, keeping the seeds close together. Fill in areas around bigger seeds with small seeds. Apply more glue as you work on the edges of the medallion. Let dry completely.

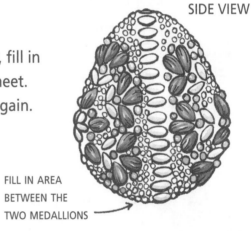

FRONT VIEW

START AT THE CENTER AND WORK OUT

3. When the egg pattern on one side is dry, cover the entire seed pattern with another coat of glue. (Don't worry if the glue looks milky at first — it will dry clear.) Let dry.

SIDE VIEW

4. Turn the dry egg over and repeat steps 2 and 3. Now, fill in the edges where the two medallion patterns don't meet. Let seeds dry and cover with a coat of glue. Let dry again.

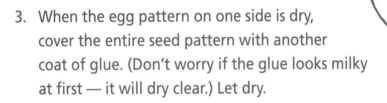

FILL IN AREA BETWEEN THE TWO MEDALLIONS

5. Fold the raffia in half. Knot the ends together. Trim, leaving about ½" (1 cm) ends. Split each end in half. Place a glob of glue at the top of the egg (the narrow end). Press the four raffia ends into the glue as shown. Let dry.

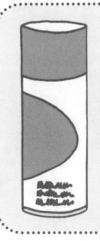

Safety First!

With adult supervision, spray the decorated egg with urethane spray, following the directions on the can and working in a well-ventilated area. Let dry.

Raffia Snowflake

In the Scandinavian countries, straw Christmas ornaments are made with pliable fresh (still green) straw that turns golden as it dries. You can get the same effect using store-bought raffia (one package will give you enough for three or four snowflakes).

❋ Materials ❋

Raffia: 20 strands, cut to 14" to 16"
    (35 to 40 cm) in length, in any color
Craft scissors
Embroidery floss of a contrasting color
Ruler
Gold thread, 12" (30 cm), for hanging

The Rap on Raffia

Working with raffia can be a bit … well, challenging. It slides and splits, and is all different thicknesses. Take your time working with it and make your ornament symmetrical by combining or splitting the raffia into equal-sized sections.

Raffia can be tied, twisted, and bent without breaking, and because it's thinner than straw, you can use several strands together. Best of all, unlike straw, raffia comes in many colors. My favorite is red raffia tied with white embroidery floss — it looks great against any evergreen!

To make the snowflake

1. Lay the raffia strands in a bundle with the ends even.

2. Cut 21 lengths of embroidery floss about 6" (15 cm) in length.

3. Use one piece of floss to tightly tie the raffia at the center point. (I like to tie three knots in the floss so it never comes undone.)

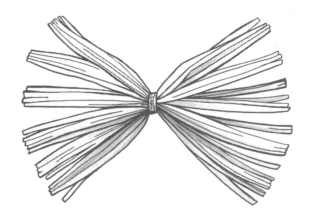

Quick Starts Tips!™

Careful measuring from each tie will help keep your ornament balanced.

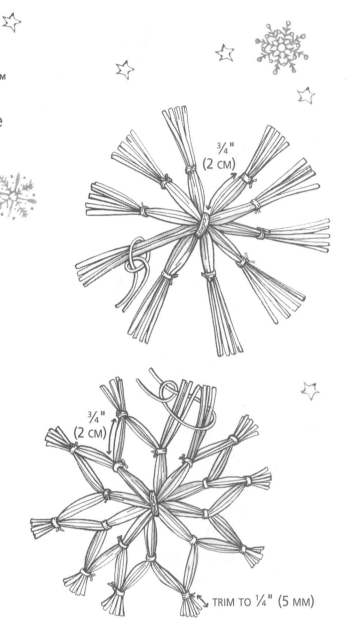

¾"
(2 CM)

¾"
(2 CM)

TRIM TO ¼" (5 MM)

4. Divide one side into five *even* sections of raffia. (The even part is important; it doesn't matter so much how many strands are in each section, but each section should be the same thickness. Split the raffia if necessary.) Tie each section tightly about ¾" (2 cm) from the center. Repeat for the other side.

5. Beginning at the top and working around the star, divide the ends in half again by thickness, splitting raffia strands if necessary. Tie each half to half of the next section about ¾" (2 cm) from the last tie, making the outer point of the star. Continue around the star, forming the remaining points. (Remember to tie each section with three knots.)

6. Adjust the star so it is symmetrical. Trim the ends about ¼" (5 mm) from the last set of ties. Thread the gold thread through one of the star points and knot, forming a hanging loop.

More Quick Starts Fun!

Gift wrap! Wrap your gifts in plain brown grocery bags or white butcher wrap, and place a red and green raffia star on top. That way, you give two gifts — one inside the box and one outside the box!

Ice Skater Ornament

OK, so this is my favorite! Why? Because I can go wild with this fun and funky ornament — and you can, too! Make the outfit totally glam or go retro!

❄ Materials ❄

Template supplies: tracing paper, craft scissors, cereal-box cardboard

Embroidery floss, two bright contrasting colors, for shirt and pants

Craft glue

Wooden clothespin (the nonspring type)

Yarn: 20" (50 cm) for the boots (or slippers) and hat; 3 yards (3 m) kinky cotton yarn for the hair

Acrylic paints and small paintbrush, for the face

Gold thread, 10" (25 cm), for hanging

Masking or duct tape (optional)

To make the ice skater

1. Trace the ICE SKATER ARM template below onto tracing paper and cut out. Then, trace two times on cardboard as shown for the actual arm pieces.

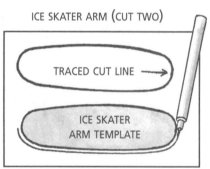

ICE SKATER ARM (CUT TWO)

TRACED CUT LINE →

ICE SKATER ARM TEMPLATE

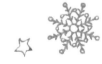

GLUE AND WRAP

2. Cut a 12" (30 cm) length of floss for the shirt. Beginning at the neck, dab glue on one side of the clothespin. Place the floss end in the glue, then wrap it from the neck of the clothespin down just beyond where the pin indents slightly. Glue the end.

3. To make the pants, dab glue on top of the last few wraps of the shirt floss and down to where the clothespin splits. Wrap contrasting floss over the first color about three turns and down to the split. Continue to glue and wrap, covering each "leg" separately. Keep the floss strands close together.

☆   ☆   ☆

4. To make the legwarmers, glue the yarn end in place, then glue and wrap from the leg down to the tip, covering the bottom of each leg. Cut and glue the end.

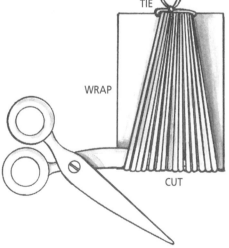

5. Use both floss colors to make striped arms. Spread glue on the cardboard "arm." Then, wrap the floss down the arm, making sure the colors stay side by side (but don't overlap), so that you get the striped pattern. Cut and glue the ends just above the hands. Repeat for the other arm. Glue each arm at the shoulder onto the clothespin skater.

6. For the hair, wrap the hair yarn about 15 times around a flat 3" (7.5 cm) length of cardboard. Tie with a piece of floss at the top. Cut the looped ends. Glue to the top of the clothespin at the tie.

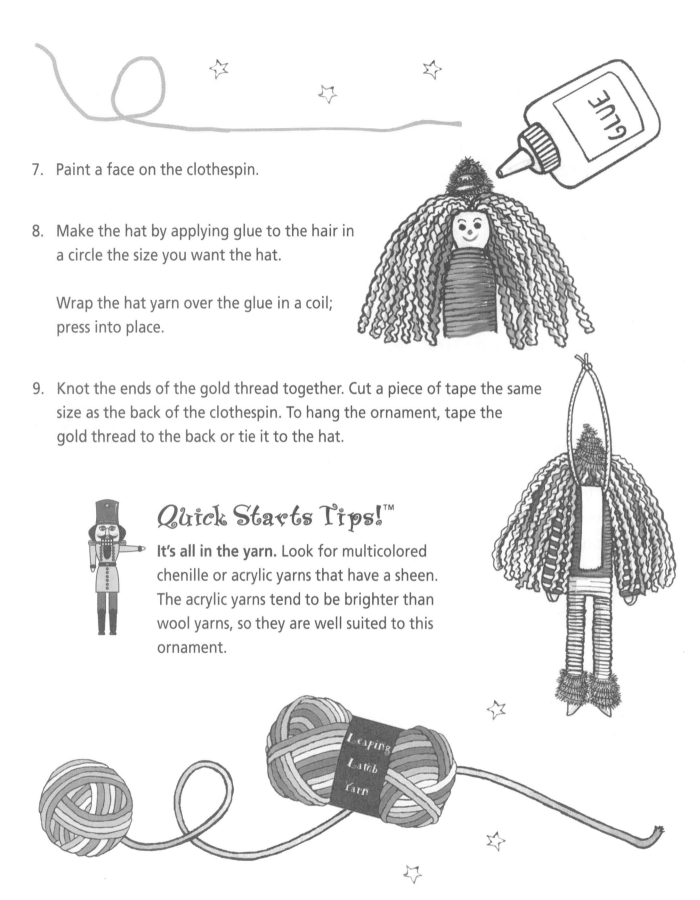

7. Paint a face on the clothespin.

8. Make the hat by applying glue to the hair in a circle the size you want the hat.

    Wrap the hat yarn over the glue in a coil; press into place.

9. Knot the ends of the gold thread together. Cut a piece of tape the same size as the back of the clothespin. To hang the ornament, tape the gold thread to the back or tie it to the hat.

Quick Starts Tips!™

It's all in the yarn. Look for multicolored chenille or acrylic yarns that have a sheen. The acrylic yarns tend to be brighter than wool yarns, so they are well suited to this ornament.

Hearts Aglow Felt Heart

This soft, two-toned stuffed felt heart is full of personality! Its fancy (but super simple) stitching takes it far beyond the typical heart ornament — it's a hanging sewing sampler! Learn how to make a French knot and embroider snowflakes in a few quick steps, then add your own touches. This also makes a great pincushion for a sewing-basket gift!

❄ Materials ❄

Template supplies: tracing paper, craft scissors, cereal-box cardboard

Pen, for tracing onto felt

Felt: two 5" (12.5 cm) squares of red; one 3" (7.5 cm) square of pink

Fabric scissors

Sewing needle with a large eye

Bright pink and light pink embroidery floss, 20" (50 cm)

Glue gun or craft glue

Straight pins

Batting or cotton balls, for stuffing

To make the heart

1. Trace the two HEART templates (page 58) onto tracing paper and cut out. Trace the templates onto cardboard, label, and cut out.

2. Trace the smaller heart pattern onto the pink felt and cut it out using fabric scissors.

3. Trace the larger heart pattern onto one red felt square and cut it out. Repeat for the second red felt square.

4. Embroider snowflakes (page 19) on the pink heart or add shapes or decorations (see *Quick Starts Tips!*™, page 18).

5. Center the decorated pink heart on top of one of the red hearts, and glue it in place. Make French knots (page 19) in the red heart, if desired.

6. Pin the two red hearts together, matching tips and curves, with the design facing out. Remove two pins on one of the sides and stuff the heart with batting or cotton balls.

   Glue the open side. Press closed. Then, removing a pin at a time, open slightly and continue to glue together on the inside. Press closed. Continue around the edge, unpinning and gluing.

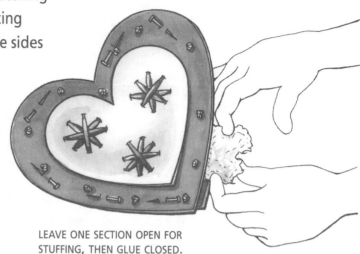

LEAVE ONE SECTION OPEN FOR STUFFING, THEN GLUE CLOSED.

7. Thread the needle with floss. Poke the needle through the top of the heart. Pull the thread halfway through and knot the ends to form a loop.

More Quick Starts Fun!

♡ Fill with balsam needles or potpourri and decorate for a scented winter heart.
♡ Decorate with hearts or flowers to make a sweet-smelling Valentine's Day or Mother's Day sachet.

Quick Starts Tips!™

Easy does it! Don't like to sew? No problem! Instead of sewing on snowflakes, glue sequins, buttons, or spirals, stars, or flowers cut from different-colored felt scraps.

Let it Snow ...
with Embroidered Snowflakes!

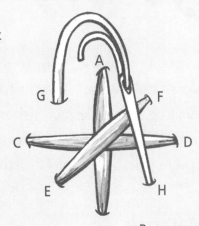

1. Thread the needle with the bright pink floss; knot one end. Bring the needle from the back side of the pink heart at A. Insert the needle at B to make one long stitch.

2. Come up at C to begin a second stitch. Once you insert the needle at D, you'll have a cross.

3. Make two more stitches slightly shorter in length as shown (come up at E, insert at F, come up at G, insert at H), forming an X over the cross.

4. Knot the end and repeat in new spots to make two more snowflakes.

5. Make French knots (see below) in the red heart.

French Knot: French knots are fun and not at all difficult to do. They add a nice decorative look, perfect for tiny buttonlike bumps or miniature eyes. Knot the thread and bring the needle up from the back of the piece to the front. Wrap the thread around the tip of the needle four times, and then insert the needle into the fabric as close as possible to the point where you came up through the fabric. Slowly pull the needle until the thread secures the four little twists. What's left will be a French knot!

Mystery-Fold Star

This one will really fool your friends! It can't be figured out unless you unwrap the star to find the start, so your secret will be safe unless you share it. These flat stars make a perfect gift to send through the mail in an envelope (a great idea for Christmas cards!).

❋ Materials ❋

Construction-paper strips, 1" x 12" (2.5 x 30 cm), two each of two contrasting colors
Pencil
Sewing needle
Gold thread, 12" (30 cm), for hanging

To make the star

1. Lay two same-color strips flat on your work surface, lining the ends up evenly. Lay the two contrasting-color strips perpendicular (at a right angle) to the first strips. Weave them together as shown, and lightly number the ends in pencil *on the front and back of the strips.*

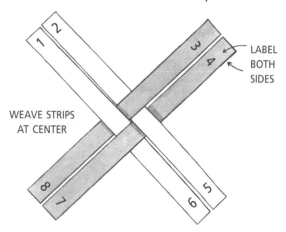

WEAVE STRIPS AT CENTER

LABEL BOTH SIDES

2. Fold end 2 down over itself with the end on top of end 5. Fold ends 4, 6, and 8 in order in the same way (4 over to 7, 6 to 1, 8 to 3). On the last fold, pull end 8 through the "pocket" formed by end 2.

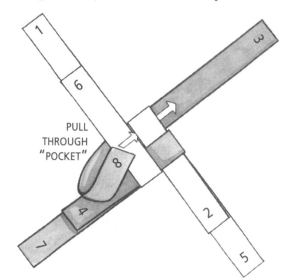

PULL THROUGH "POCKET"

3. Flip the star over. Fold end 5, then 3, 1, and 7, pulling end 7 through the pocket formed by end 5 to lock it in place. At this point, all the strips should be the same length again.

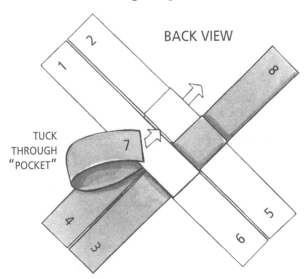

BACK VIEW

TUCK THROUGH "POCKET"

4. Renumber the ends front and back 1 to 8 as before. Fold end 2 *at a right angle* so the end lands parallel (side by side) to end 3. Repeat with ends 4, 6, and 8.

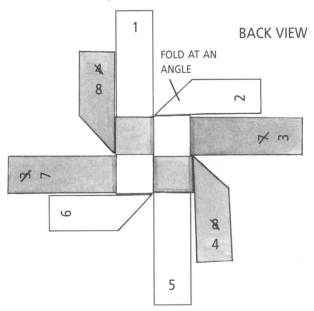

BACK VIEW

FOLD AT AN ANGLE

5. Flip the star over and fold ends 8, 6, 4, and 2 again, forming points.

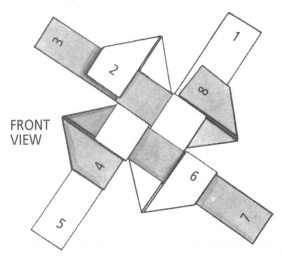

FRONT VIEW

6. Now fold the points closed and tuck the ends into the closest pockets. You now have four completed points.

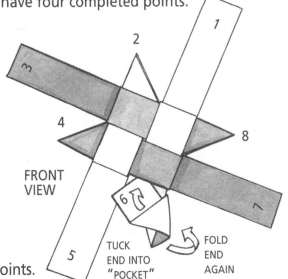

FRONT VIEW

TUCK END INTO "POCKET"

FOLD END AGAIN

7. Repeat steps 4, 5, and 6 to form the last four star points.

8. Thread the needle with the gold thread. Poke the needle through the paper between two points of the same color. Pull the thread about halfway through and knot the two ends to make a loop. Hang your ornament and be ready for many compliments!

"NOT A CREATURE WAS STIRRING"

Gossamer-Wing Bead Dragonfly

Delicate see-through fabric or ribbon and light beads give this airy dragonfly ornament its wonderful iridescence. When hung, it looks as if it's just alighting momentarily on your tree!

❋ Materials ❋

Choose your own colors or use those suggested here.

Green plastic-coated craft wire or floral wire, two 9" (22.5 cm) pieces for the body; one 4" (10 cm) piece to attach the wings

Craft scissors, for cutting wire

Wire-edged metallic ribbon, blue and lavender, one 4" (10 cm) long and one 5½" (14 cm) long, for the wings

Beads, with holes large enough to fit a double strand of wire:

    2 opalescent blues or greens, for the head

    2 opalescent ⅜" (7.5 mm) diamond shapes, for the eyes

    8 opalescent blues or greens, for the thorax

    14 opalescent ¼" (5 mm) browns, for the abdomen

    6 small (⅛"/2.5 mm) green or blue glass beads, for the legs

Gold thread, 10" (25 cm), for hanging

To make the dragonfly

1. Pass the two longer wires through the first head bead, leaving about an inch (2.5 cm) extension for the antennae. Separate the wires beneath the bead. Slide an eye bead onto each wire. Bring the wires back together, and pass them in opposite directions through the remaining head bead (the left wire passes to the right, the right wire passes through to the left). Pull the wires tight.

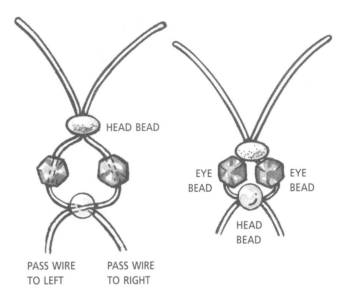

HEAD BEAD

EYE BEAD

EYE BEAD

HEAD BEAD

PASS WIRE TO LEFT

PASS WIRE TO RIGHT

2. To make the thorax, slide four beads onto each wire. Bring the wires together and twist twice, forming a small oval.

3. To make the abdomen and legs, slide seven beads onto each wire. Add three small blue or green glass leg beads to each wire. Trim the wires, twisting each end around the last bead on the wire.

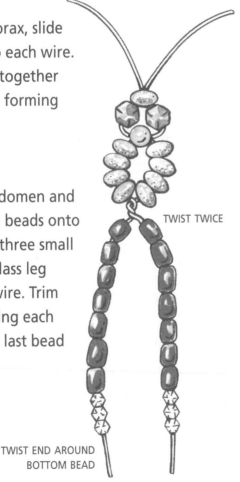

TWIST TWICE

TWIST END AROUND BOTTOM BEAD

Quick Starts Tips!™

The bead on beads. Craft stores sell small quantities of beads grouped by colors and size. One package of ¼" (5 mm) beads for the body and different colors for the head work well, plus a few special accent beads for the eyes and small glass seed beads for the legs. Anything goes, but make sure a double strand of the craft or florist wire will fit through the bead hole.

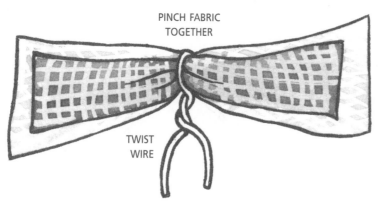

PINCH FABRIC
TOGETHER

TWIST
WIRE

4. To make the wings, layer the shorter fabric or ribbon on top of the longer one. Pinch together at the center. Fold the small wire in half and fasten tightly around the wings. Then, cross and twist the extra wire on the underside of the wings.

5. Hold the two wire ends together and pass them through the thorax. Twist the wires once, then separate them and wrap each end around the body wire next to the second bead on each side. Turn the dragonfly over and adjust the wings.

TWIST WIRES
TOGETHER ONCE

TWIST EACH END AROUND
THE BODY WIRE

6. Tie the gold thread to the base of the thorax and double-knot it at the back. Extend the ends above the dragonfly and knot again. Twist each end of the antennae into a small loop.

Starfish Snowman

Starfish and snowmen don't seem to have much in common, but with a little imagination, you can turn this textured salt dough into anything from a funny snowman to beautiful, glittering starfish. You decide!

❋ Materials ❋

Template supplies: tracing paper, craft
    scissors, cereal-box cardboard
Salt dough (see recipe, page 26)
Waxed paper, to protect your work surface
Rolling pin (optional)
Dull knife, for cutting dough
Cookie sheet
Small gravel or clean kitty litter, about
    2 tablespoons (25 ml) per starfish
White, black, and orange acrylic paints and
    paintbrush
Ribbon, 18" (45 cm) long, ½" (1 cm) wide
        Black felt scrap and
            glue, for the hat
        Gold thread, 16"
            (40 cm), for hanging

To make the starfish

1. Trace the four STARFISH templates (page 60) onto tracing paper and cut out. Then, trace onto cardboard, label, and cut out.

Quick Starts Tips!™

Use the tracing-paper starfish as the actual pattern for this ornament because it sticks slightly to the dough, making it easier to cut around the pattern shape. You'll want to make the cardboard pattern, too, though, so you'll have a permanent starfish pattern on hand for future ornaments.

2. Make the salt dough.

3. Divide the dough into five or six balls (each ball will use about ⅓ cup/ 75 ml of dough). On waxed paper, flatten the ball with your hands or roll out with a rolling pin to about 6" (15 cm) in diameter. The dough should be about ¼" (5 mm) in thickness.

4. Place the starfish pattern on top of the dough and cut around it with the kitchen knife. Gently remove the excess dough.

5. Transfer the starfish to the cookie sheet. Repeat the process to make more starfish, but leave some dough to make faces and buttons.

6. Sprinkle the gravel over the dough. Do it *lightly*, because gravel is difficult to remove once it's on! Once you have the texture you want, press the gravel into the dough enough to make it stick.

Salt Dough

1⅓ cups (325 ml) flour
1½ cups (375 ml) salt
Cooking oil
Large bowl
Water
Spoon
Zip-locking plastic bag

1. Mix the flour, salt, and a few drops of cooking oil together in the large bowl. Add ½ cup (125 ml) water. Stir with a spoon until it makes soft dough. Add more water if it is too dry and a bit of flour if it gets too sticky.
2. Press and squeeze (knead) the dough with your hands until it forms a ball.
3. Store the dough in the plastic bag until you are ready to use it.
4. To use, shape the dough and bake at 170°F (77°C) for about three hours. When done, the baked dough should "ping" when tapped with your fingernail or a spoon — similar to the sound you get when you tap china.

Quick Starts Tips!™

It's not too late! If you baked the starfish without pressing gravel into the dough, you can still apply gravel. Paint the surface of the baked starfish with a layer of white glue. Spread gravel over this surface and let dry. Paint over the gravel texture. Or add glitter to the wet paint (page 27).

7. Roll the last bits of dough into tiny balls for the eyes and pointy nose. Add three balls for the buttons. Place the tray of shapes into the oven and bake according to the recipe.

8. When the dough is cool, paint the starfish white. Let dry. Paint the eyes and buttons black, and the nose orange. Allow paint to dry. Tie the ribbon around the snowman's "neck."

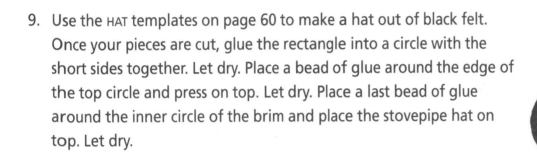

GLUE HERE

GLUE HERE

9. Use the HAT templates on page 60 to make a hat out of black felt. Once your pieces are cut, glue the rectangle into a circle with the short sides together. Let dry. Place a bead of glue around the edge of the top circle and press on top. Let dry. Place a last bead of glue around the inner circle of the brim and place the stovepipe hat on top. Let dry.

10. Tie the gold thread around the snowman's neck to hang your ornament.

More Quick Starts Fun!

Images from the sea. Instead of a snowman, make a natural-looking painted starfish to hang on your tree using acrylic paints and glitter. Follow the recipe and directions for making the Starfish Snowman, but omit the face and buttons. Be sure to make a hole in the dough at the top of one "arm" for the hanger. Bake according to directions.

When the salt clay is hard and cool, paint the starfish on both sides with tan paint. To make a nice starfish color, mix a small amount of blue with red, yellow, and white paints. Highlight areas by dabbing orange over the wet surface. Let sit about five minutes. While the surface is still wet, sprinkle with purple, pink, and white glitters. Or, try your own color combinations!

Let dry. Then thread embroidery floss or gold cord through the hole and hang from a strong branch. Decorate the tree with other ocean images or paint clean, empty shells in sea colors or pastels and hang with thin twine (just tap a hole with a nail and hammer).

Feather Bird

If you love birds, you'll be pleased to know that you can create a whole flock with just one bag of craft feathers. Choose your color combinations — either imaginary or true to nature — and then let them soar!

❈ Materials ❈

Template supplies: tracing paper, craft scissors, cereal-box cardboard

Poster board or cardboard for the backing (see box)

Craft feathers

Craft glue

Scrap of yellow paper, for the beak

Wiggle eyes

Lightweight wire or pipe cleaner, 4" (10 cm) of any color, for the feet

Tape

Ribbon, 10" (25 cm), for hanging

To make the bird

1. Trace the BIRD template (page 59) onto tracing paper and cut out. Then, trace onto cardboard, mark the eye, label, and cut out.

2. Trace the pattern onto the backing. Cut it out.

3. Select feathers (this is the fun part!) and separate by size and color. Save the smallest feathers for the head. Cover the bird with glue (I like to spread it with my finger for best results). Beginning with the tail section, place one feather at a time, pointing the hard end onto the backing and the "feathery" part out. Press in place.

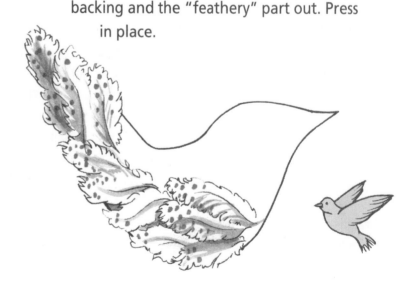

4. Continue placing feathers, overlapping the feathers as you go, working down the tail and across the body to the head. Add a wiggle eye and beak.

5. Fold the wire or pipe cleaner in half, then twist it. Bend it in half again with a slight separation. Place the bent wire on the back of the bird so that two "feet" extend below the bottom, set apart at the distance you want. Tape it onto the cardboard. Bend the wire out at the ends so you have feet.

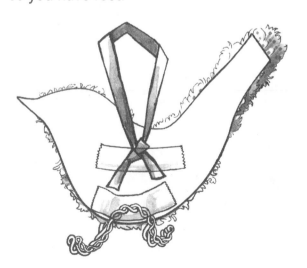

6. Make a loop with the ribbon and tie in a knot. Tape the knot to the back of the bird, making sure the bird will hang straight.

7. Cover the back of the bird with feathers, a beak, and a wiggle eye in the same way, if you like, or leave it as is.

More Quick Starts Fun!

Feed the birds. When the holidays have passed and your bird ornaments are tucked away until next year, put your tree and your template to good use.

Stand the tree up outdoors in an open area where feeding birds will be safe from predators (like hungry cats!).

Trace your bird template onto light cardboard or poster board. Cut out, punch a hole, and tie on a ribbon or string. Then, slather on some peanut butter and add birdseed or sunflower seeds (a bird favorite). Now watch the birds enjoy a post-holiday feast!

Buzzing Bee

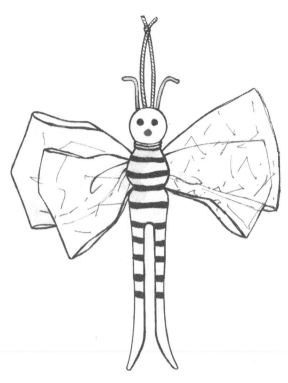

What's the "buzz"? Your holiday decorations, that's what! This cheerful ornament, with its yellow and black striped and shiny wings, can dangle from a tree branch or sit atop a special package under the tree!

❄ Materials ❄

Wooden clothespin (the nonspring type)

Yellow and black acrylic paint and small paintbrush, for the stripes

Toothpick, for painting eye and mouth details

Scissors

Clear plastic wrap or plastic bag

Yellow or black wire, 6" (15 cm), to secure wings and make the antennae

Gold thread, 10" (25 cm), for hanging

To make the bee

1. Paint the clothespin bright yellow. Let dry.

2. Paint black stripes around the body and down each leg of the clothespin. Paint two small black eyes and a dot for the mouth on the head of the pin.

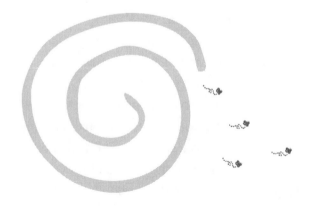

Quick Starts Tips!™

Quick work. Work quickly when painting or using marker on wooden beads or clothespins, as too much ink or paint may "bleed," or spread slightly across the wood.

3. Cut a piece of plastic that's 2" x 9" (5 x 22.5 cm) and fold it in half, matching short ends. Twist the wire tightly around the middle of the plastic.

4. Place the wings on the back of the clothespin. Separate the wire, bringing both ends around to the front. Overlap the wires at the front and continue around to the back. Twist to secure.

5. Separate the wires at the back of the head. Bend up into antennae. Clip ends to the same length.

6. Slide the gold thread under the antennae wire; tie in a knot. Hang your bee high in the branches of your tree!

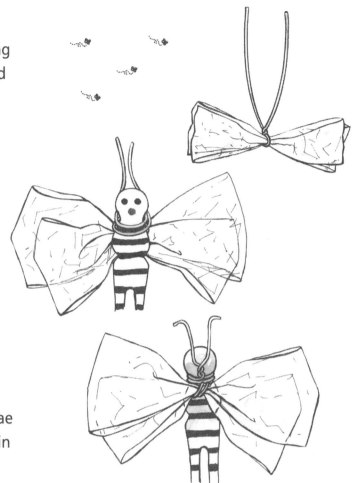

More Quick Starts Fun!

Host a clothespin ornament–making party. On one of those "I can't wait 'til Christmas" days, invite a few friends over for ornament fun. Put out acrylic paints, paintbrushes, a bag of wooden clothespins (nonspring type), lots of trims, felt scraps, and mini pom-poms, and then let the fun begin! You can start with this toy soldier and Raggedy Andy, plus the Ice Skater on page 14 (they all use the same ARM template). Then, let your imagination do its own thing! Oh yes, don't forget the cocoa and Christmas cookies!

POM-POMS

GOLD THREAD EPAULETS

PAINT DETAILS

Christmas Hobby Horse

Bright-colored felt brings this little horse to life! With a fringed mane, a glitter bridle, and gold reins, this Christmas ornament is all set to hold a candy cane and prance among the branches of your tree!

❄ Materials ❄

Template supplies: tracing paper, craft scissors, cereal-box cardboard

Felt: 4" x 8" (10 x 20 cm) of a bright color, plus a scrap of black

Straight pins

Pen, for tracing on felt

Looped fringe, 4" (10 cm), black or other color

Glue gun

Wiggle eyes

Gold glitter

Gold cord

Curved candy cane

Quick Starts Tips!™

Fringe fun. Don't have fringe on hand? Make your own. Loop black yarn around a 1" x 4" (2.5 x 10 cm) piece of cardboard. Without taking the fringe off the card, glue along the top side of the fringe with a glue gun so that it forms a solid edge. Let dry, then carefully slip the fringe off the card and place on the felt horse.

To make the horse

1. Trace the two HOBBY HORSE templates (page 58) onto tracing paper. Mark the two dots and cut out. Trace the templates onto cardboard, transfer the markings, label, and cut out.

2. Fold the felt in half with short sides together. Pin to hold in place. Trace the pattern onto the felt with the pen. Leaving the pins in place, use the fabric scissors to cut inside the lines through both layers so markings don't show.

3. Place the fringe on top of one felt horse, between the dots so it extends about ½" (1 cm) above the horse shape. Pin in place with several pins. Removing a pin at a time, open slightly and glue together on the inside. Press closed. Continue down the edge, unpinning and gluing.

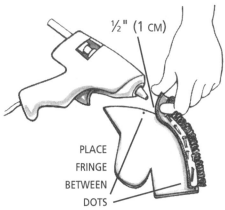

½" (1 CM)

PLACE FRINGE BETWEEN DOTS

4. Place the other felt horse piece over the glued fringed felt and pin in place at several places, matching edges and points. Removing a pin at a time, open slightly and glue together on the inside. Press closed. Continue unpinning and gluing. Leave the bottom open.

5. Cut out an eye background from the black felt. Glue in place on the front of the horse. Glue the wiggle eye on top of the felt. Use glue to make a bridle. Sprinkle with glitter or press on pieces of gold cord, cut to fit. Repeat on the other side if you want a two-sided horse face and bridle. Tuck a candy cane inside and tie on gold cord to hang.

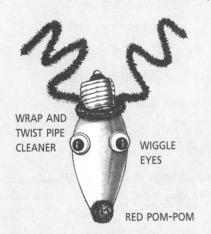

WIGGLE EYE

BLACK FELT

GLITTER BRIDLE

More Quick Starts Fun!

Make a reindeer bulb. Try this quick craft for some more prancing fun! It's perfect for an ornament-making party with your friends (page 31), too. The large colored Christmas tree bulbs can be purchased in a set with different colors. (I find the elongated 3" to 4"/8 to 10 cm bulbs work best.) Or, recycle the burned-out bulbs from your tree! To turn your reindeer into a pin to wear on a coat instead, omit the hanger and hot-glue a pin closure to the back.

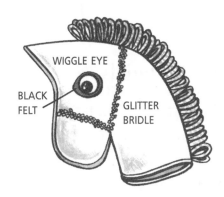

WRAP AND TWIST PIPE CLEANER

WIGGLE EYES

RED POM-POM

Wrap a brown pipe cleaner around the socket end of the lightbulb, twisting it tightly in the back. Bend ends into zigzag antler shapes. Glue two wiggle eyes in place, holding them until set so they won't slip. Glue a ½" (1 cm) red or black pom-pom to the end of the bulb. To hang it up, tie gold thread around the neck of the ornament and knot the ends. Twist the gold thread through the antlers so that your reindeer hangs straight.

Stuffed Teddy Bear

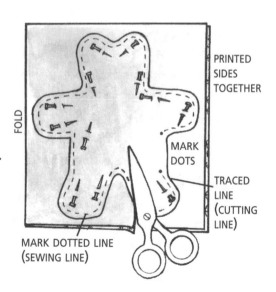

This little bear is a snap to make, even if you've never sewn before. The one here is made out of cotton calico, but you can use any fabric you like — even soft felt or corduroy. Deck it out in a fancy bow and give your teddy some eyes and a nose, if you like! My teddy is filled with batting, but for a sweet-smelling bear sachet, fill yours with holiday potpourri or balsam needles.

❄ Materials ❄

Template supplies: tracing paper, craft scissors, cereal-box cardboard
Sewing supplies: pen, straight pins, fabric scissors, sewing needle
Print or solid cotton fabric, 7" x 14" (17.5 x 35 cm), with matching thread
Batting or cotton balls, for stuffing
Ribbon, ½" x 18" (1 x 45 cm)
Embroidery floss, 16" (40 cm), for hanging

To make the bear

1. Trace the TEDDY BEAR template (page 61) and markings onto tracing paper and cut out. Trace the template onto cardboard, label, and cut out. Mark the two small dots and the ¼" (5 mm) sewing line.

2. Fold the fabric as shown, with the fabric's printed (or good) sides together (on the inside). Trace the pattern onto the fabric and transfer all markings.

3. Pin through both layers of fabric to hold in place. Use fabric scissors to cut along the solid traced line, cutting out two fabric bears.

FOLD

PRINTED SIDES TOGETHER

MARK DOTS

TRACED LINE (CUTTING LINE)

MARK DOTTED LINE (SEWING LINE)

4. Thread the needle and knot the end. With the two bear pieces still pinned with printed sides together, take a stitch at the dot under the bear's arm through both layers of fabric. Sew with a running stitch (below) ¼" (5 mm) in from the outer edge of the fabric, all the way around the bear's body, ending at the second dot. Knot and snip the thread; remove any pins.

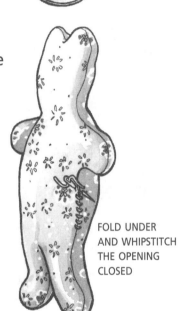

¼" (5 MM)

START HERE

END HERE; KNOT AND SNIP

5. To turn the bear so the printed sides are out, pull the printed side of the fabric through the opening left between the two dots. Use a pencil to push out the fabric in the legs, ears, arms, and feet.

6. Lightly stuff the bear, using the pencil to poke the stuffing into the head and ends of the body. Fill the body cavity last.

7. Fold the fabric edges into the side opening and pin in place. Thread a needle and knot the long end. Hide the knot inside the bear and whipstitch (below) the opening closed.

8. Tie the ribbon into a bow at the neck. Trim the ends. Thread the needle with the floss. Poke the needle through the top of the bear's head. Pull the floss halfway through and knot the two ends to make a loop.

FOLD UNDER AND WHIPSTITCH THE OPENING CLOSED

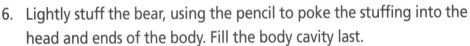

Running Stitch: This stitch is great for making seams. Knot the thread and bring the needle up through. Work the tip of the needle in and out of the fabric to create three or four stitches and then pull the thread through. Continue this way until you finish the seam.

Whipstitch: The whipstitch is used to join two finished edges. Bring the needle from the WRONG side of the fabric to the RIGHT side to hide the knot in your thread. Now, wrap the thread across the two fabric pieces. Continue wrapping stitches over the seam until the seam is sewn.

TRIM THE TREE!

Jolly Old St. Nick

No tree is complete without a Santa! This jolly St. Nick is made out of craft foam, so it's super-simple to cut, assemble, and glue. Decorate Santa's suit with stars or sequins, add a gold cord for his belt, and put a star on his cap. An added plus: This flat ornament can be slipped into an envelope and sent through the mail — guaranteed not to crush!

❄ Materials ❄

Template supplies: tracing paper, craft
　　scissors, cereal-box cardboard
Craft foam: 6" (15 cm) square of red for the
　　body; scraps of white for the face and
　　beard, black for the boots, and yellow
　　for the star
Craft glue
Twisted gold cord, 18" (45 cm) for the belt;
　　12" (30 cm), for hanging
Sequins, stars, or other trims, for decorations
Paper punch (optional)
Fine-tip red marker
Large needle or small nail

To make the Santa

1. Trace the four JOLLY OLD ST. NICK templates (page 62) onto tracing paper and cut out. Then, trace onto cardboard, label, and cut out.

2. Trace each cardboard pattern onto its color of craft foam. Cut out the shapes.

3. Position Santa's face and beard, the yellow star at the top and the boots on the bottom.

(You'll need to turn one of the boots over so it covers the star shape tip as shown.) Glue all the pieces in place; let dry.

4. Tie the gold cord around Santa's waist and make a bow. Trim and knot each end.

5. Glue sequins or stars on the red Santa suit.

6. Punch out two round eyes from a scrap of black craft foam. Glue in place. Add a small mouth with red marker.

7. Poke the needle or nail through the top of the Santa just above the star (or through the star). Pull the cord about halfway through the hole and knot the ends together.

Quick Starts Tips!™

Save those patterns! Save all the cardboard patterns in a zip-locking plastic bag. Make sure each piece is labeled with the ornament name and the part (St. Nick/boots).

More Quick Starts Fun!

Make other holiday-shaped ornaments out of different colors of craft foam. Either trace shapes around cookie cutters or draw your own. Decorate with colorful foam scraps, sparkles, sequins, or glass beads.

Holly Leaf Elf

"Oh, the holly and the ivy …" This adorable felt holly elf is held together with a piece of pipe cleaner. Let it peek out from the tree's branches or attach it to a small, but special, package.

❄ Materials ❄

Template supplies: tracing paper, craft scissors, cereal-box cardboard

Pen, for tracing onto felt

Felt: 4" (10 cm) square of green for the leaves; scrap of red for the berries

Fabric scissors

Black and red acrylic paint and small paintbrush, for the face

Wooden bead for the head

Pipe cleaner, 6" (15 cm)

Gold thread, 10" (25 cm), for hanging

Craft glue

To make the elf

1. Trace the three HOLLY LEAF ELF templates (page 39) onto tracing paper and cut out. Then, trace onto cardboard, label, and cut out.

2. Use the pen to trace the pattern pieces onto the green felt. Cut out.

3. Paint a face onto the wooden bead. Let dry.

 **Quick Starts Tips!™**

Scissors! Remember: Craft scissors cut paper; fabric scissors cut fabrics. Don't mix them up or you'll have good-for-nothing scissors. OK?

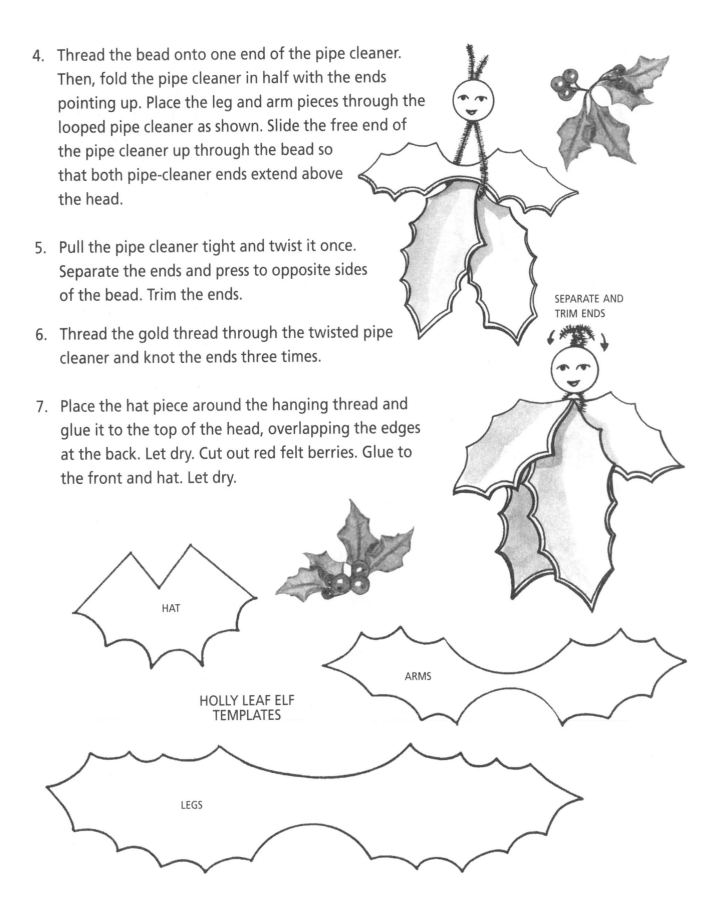

4. Thread the bead onto one end of the pipe cleaner. Then, fold the pipe cleaner in half with the ends pointing up. Place the leg and arm pieces through the looped pipe cleaner as shown. Slide the free end of the pipe cleaner up through the bead so that both pipe-cleaner ends extend above the head.

5. Pull the pipe cleaner tight and twist it once. Separate the ends and press to opposite sides of the bead. Trim the ends.

6. Thread the gold thread through the twisted pipe cleaner and knot the ends three times.

7. Place the hat piece around the hanging thread and glue it to the top of the head, overlapping the edges at the back. Let dry. Cut out red felt berries. Glue to the front and hat. Let dry.

SEPARATE AND TRIM ENDS

HAT

HOLLY LEAF ELF TEMPLATES

ARMS

LEGS

Quilled Christmas Poinsettia

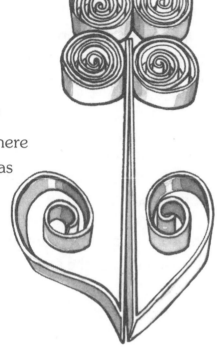

Poinsettias (poyn-SET-ee-ahs) are known as the flower of Christmas, a tradition that traveled north from Mexico, where they are called *La Flor de Noche Buena,* or The Christmas Eve Flower. According to legend, a poor Mexican child knelt in a church on Christmas Eve, praying for a gift to offer the Christ Child. Miraculously, a poinsettia sprang up at the child's feet. And that is why you may want to make this delicate poinsettia made from *quilled* paper (narrow rolled strips) to adorn a tree or gift!

❆ Materials ❆

Ruler

Pencil

Craft scissors

Red and green construction
     paper

Toothpick, for curling

Craft glue

Embroidery floss or gold
     thread, 10" (25 cm),
     for hanging

To make the poinsettia

1. Mark and cut the paper into four red and two green ¼" x 12" (5 mm x 30 cm) strips.

2. Roll each red section around the toothpick as tightly as you can. Remove the toothpick and place a dot of glue on the end of each curl. Press. You'll have four red quilled circles.

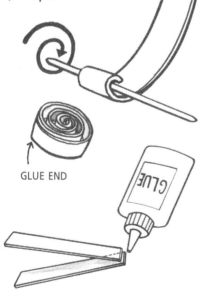

GLUE END

3. Glue the two green strips together at one end. Hold the stems in place until dry.

Quick Starts Tips!™

Curl up. To make a fatter quilled circle, wrap your paper around a wider base. You can use nails, small paintbrush handles, and pencils for different curl sizes.

4. Glue the red curls together around the glued end of the green strips as shown.

5. About halfway down the stem on both sides, fold the ends up. Loosely curl the leaves with the pencil. Glue the base of the stem together. Let dry.

6. Thread the embroidery floss or thread through the center of the flower. Knot the ends together to hang.

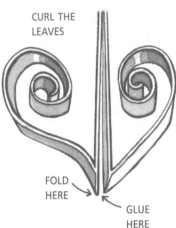

CURL THE LEAVES

FOLD HERE

GLUE HERE

More Quick Starts Fun!

Larger poinsettias? To make larger poinsettias, you can glue more curled circles around the outside of the four circles you have now. Or, to make another kind of flower, simply change the shape, size, and color of the quilled circles. You'll be amazed at the flowers you can make all year round.

Quilled Snowflake

The small quilled circles in this delicate snowflake are easy to make (that's what's so cool about it — it just *looks* hard!). Try it with plain white or pastel-colored paper, or make your own watercolor-designed papers. Add a shimmer of glitter so your snowflake will glisten on the tree. Once you've made one, make a whole snowstorm — but remember that Mother Nature never makes two snowflakes alike, so try some variations.

❄ Materials ❄

Ruler

Pencil

Craft scissors

Construction paper

Toothpick, for gluing

Craft glue

Small lid or plate, for gluing
   (optional)

Silver glitter (optional)

Embroidery floss or thread,
   10" (25 cm), for hanging

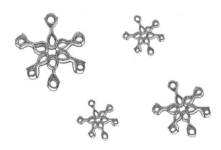

To make the snowflake

1. Mark and cut the paper into three ¼" x 10" (5 mm x 25 cm) strips. From the first paper strip, mark and then cut six 1½" (4 cm) sections (you'll have about an inch/2.5 cm left over). Roll each section as tightly as you can around the pencil. Remove the pencil and place a dot of glue on the end of each strip. Press together. You'll have six circles.

1½" (4 CM)

¼" {
(5 MM)

CUT INTO SIX SECTIONS

ROLL TIGHTLY TO FORM THE
CIRCLES; GLUE OVERLAPPED ENDS

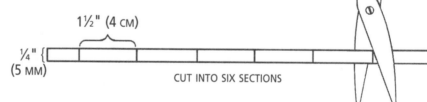

2. From the two remaining strips, mark and cut six 2¼" (5.5 cm) sections. Center each section around the pencil and pinch the ends together as shown. Remove the pencil. Glue the paper where it was pinched together; hold in place until the glue dries. You'll now have six pinched circles.

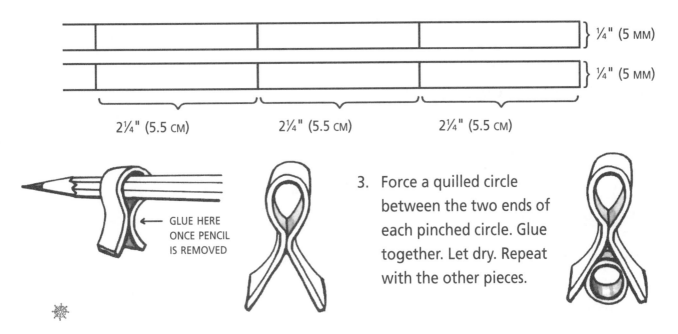

¼" (5 MM)

¼" (5 MM)

2¼" (5.5 CM)   2¼" (5.5 CM)   2¼" (5.5 CM)

GLUE HERE
ONCE PENCIL
IS REMOVED

3. Force a quilled circle between the two ends of each pinched circle. Glue together. Let dry. Repeat with the other pieces.

4. Glue together the six sections you just made as shown, so that each section touches the other sections. (You'll have a small hole left in the center.) Let dry.

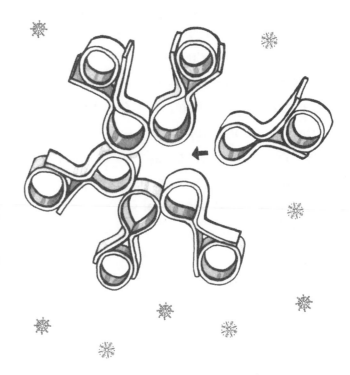

5. Spread a thin layer of glue across the lid or plate. Press the snowflake into the glue. Sprinkle glitter over the glue and let dry. Shake off any loose glitter.

6. Thread the embroidery floss or thread through one circle and knot the ends together to hang.

Bendable Felt Angel

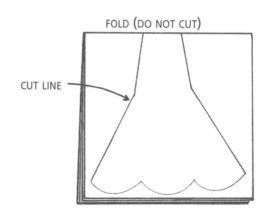

A hidden wire under the soft felt is the secret that makes this soft little angel's wings bend in flight! The delicate stitching around the edges is a cinch to do, and small painted wooden beads add a nice detail. I like to leave my angels faceless, but you can easily add a cherub face if you like, using a fine-tipped paintbrush and acrylic paints.

❄ Materials ❄

Template supplies: tracing paper, craft scissors, cereal-box cardboard

Sewing supplies: pen, fabric scissors, straight pins, needle with a large eye

Felt: 5" x 9" (12.5 x 22.5 cm) piece of pink for the dress and hat; 5" x 6" (12.5 x 15 cm) piece of white for the wings

Pipe cleaners: 3" (7.5 cm) white or light color for attaching the head; 4" (10 cm) gold-foil pipe cleaner for the halo

Beads: one large wooden bead for the head; about 12 smaller decorative beads for hands and dress decorations

Pink embroidery floss

Craft glue

Batting or cotton balls, for stuffing

Lightweight wire, 14" (35 cm)

Gold thread, 10" (25 cm), for hanging

To make the angel

1. Trace the three FELT ANGEL templates (page 59) onto tracing paper and cut out. Then, trace onto cardboard, label, and cut out.

2. Fold the pink felt in half with short sides together. Place the dress pattern against the fold line and trace onto the felt. Cut it out, cutting through both layers (do not cut along the fold). Save the scraps for the hat.

FOLD (DO NOT CUT)

CUT LINE →

3. Cut two very small clips into the felt at the fold.

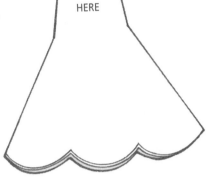

4. Thread one end of the white pipe cleaner down through the first hole and up through the second hole, making the ends even.

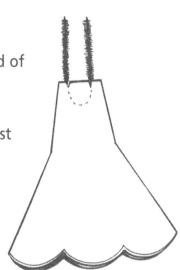

5. Thread the wooden bead onto both pipe-cleaner ends. Pull the pipe cleaner tight so the bead rests on the dress. Twist once. Separate the pipe-cleaner ends and press to opposite sides of the bead. Trim the ends.

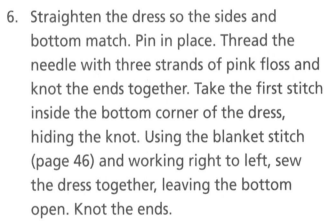

6. Straighten the dress so the sides and bottom match. Pin in place. Thread the needle with three strands of pink floss and knot the ends together. Take the first stitch inside the bottom corner of the dress, hiding the knot. Using the blanket stitch (page 46) and working right to left, sew the dress together, leaving the bottom open. Knot the ends.

7. Sew or glue beads to the outside of the dress. Arranging beads in groups of three makes a balanced design. Stuff batting or cotton balls inside the dress so it puffs out.

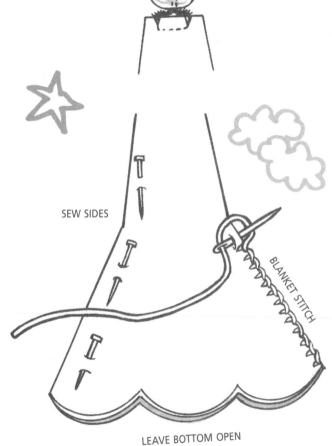

8. Fold the white felt in half with the long sides together. Trace the wing pattern and cut out. Pin the two wing pieces together. Thread the needle with three strands of pink floss, knot the ends, and sew the wings together on all sides, using the blanket stitch. Knot ends.

9. Fold the wire in half. Keeping the ends together, thread the wire through the wings so the two ends of the wire extend at one wing tip and the fold extends at the other end.

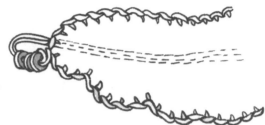

10. For the hands, thread one to three beads onto the double wire ends at both wing tips. Push the wires back into each wing tip.

11. Trace the hat pattern onto a scrap of pink felt and cut out. Wrap the hat around the wooden head, overlapping the back edges. Glue in place. Let dry.

12. Make a circle at one end of the gold pipe cleaner for the halo. Bend the pipe cleaner down and glue it to the back of the hat. Thread the needle with the gold thread. Poke the needle through the tip of the hat. Pull the thread about halfway through and knot the ends together.

Blanket Stitch: This is a great stitch for finishing raw edges in a beautiful design. Knot the thread and bring the needle up at A (along the lower line). Insert the needle at B and point it straight down. Come up again at C, this time making sure that the previous thread is *under* the needle as shown. Pull the stitch tight. The thread at C becomes the new A. Insert the needle again at a new B to continue the same pattern.

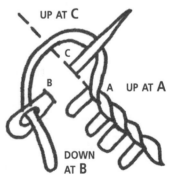

UP AT C

UP AT A

DOWN AT B

Swedish Woven Heart Basket

A tree isn't complete without a heart! The best part about this heart is its many uses. After Christmas, fill it with chocolate kisses on Valentine's Day, flowers for the perfect May Day basket, and place a sachet inside one to hang in your closet. Or, fill it with some dried flowers and give it to someone who is sick. For the best effect, use bright contrasting colors so the pattern shows.

❄ Materials ❄

Template supplies: tracing paper, ruler, craft scissors, cereal-box cardboard

Fabric: two 7" x 9" (15 x 22.5 cm) pieces of cotton, in contrasting colors or patterns

Double-faced fusible interfacing (available from craft or fabric store), two 3" x 9" (7.5 x 22.5 cm) pieces

Iron (use with adult supervision)

Pen

Fabric scissors

Narrow ribbon, 12" (30 cm), for hanging

Quick Starts Tips!™

Six hearts are better than one. If you'll be buying the cotton fabric, purchase about a ¼ yard (22.5 cm) of each color or pattern. That will give you enough fabric to make about six finished woven hearts, or more, depending on the width of the fabric. The fabric needs to be lightweight so that it's easy to cut when "sandwiched" with the interfacing. If you use holiday fabrics that have gold thread in them, use a "pressing cloth" (a cotton pillowcase or fabric scrap) over the fabric so that the metallic thread doesn't melt onto the iron.

To make the basket shapes

1. Trace the WOVEN HEART BASKET template (page 57) onto tracing paper, using a ruler to make the inner lines straight. Cut out, folding in half to cut the center lines. Then, trace onto the cardboard, label, and cut out.

2. Fold one piece of your fabric in half the long way, with the colorful side of your fabric facing out. Place the fusible interfacing into the fold between the fabric. Iron according to the interfacing directions.

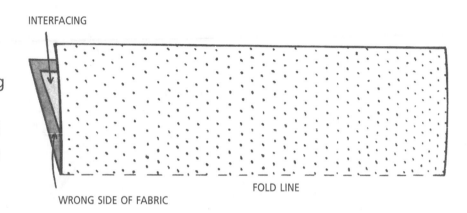

INTERFACING

WRONG SIDE OF FABRIC

FOLD LINE

3. Repeat step 2 with your other fabric. At this point, you will have two fabric strips with the interfacing inside.

4. Place the pattern on top of one fabric piece and trace around it on all the lines, including the slits in the middle. Cut the shape out just inside the lines so your markings don't show. Fold in half to cut the slit lines.

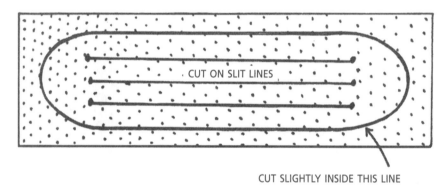

CUT ON SLIT LINES

CUT SLIGHTLY INSIDE THIS LINE

5. Repeat step 4 with the other piece of fabric.

To weave the basket together

This will take some time, so relax! The main point is that to weave the two basket sections together, you go *through* the strips, rather than over and under them.

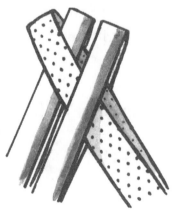

1. To weave the shapes together, fold each section in half as shown. Hold one in your left hand with the curved ends closest to your body. Hold the other in your right hand. Position the strips at a right angle to each other.

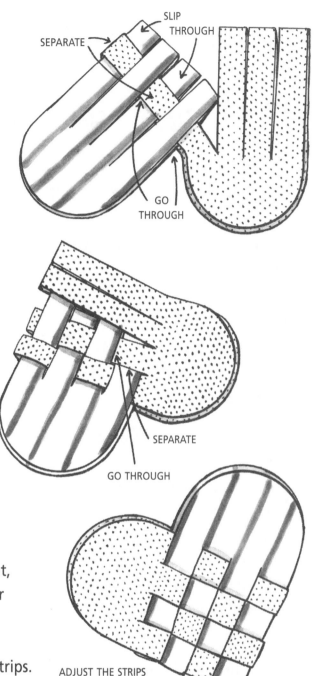

SLIP THROUGH

SEPARATE

GO THROUGH

2. I like to hold the left-hand strips stationary and weave the right-hand strips *over* and *through* them. First, weave the bottom strip in your right hand: Go *through* the first left-hand strip. *Separate* your working (right-hand) strip and slip it over the next stationary strip. Now go *through* the third, *separate*, and over the last stationary strip (so the stationary strip goes *through* it).

SEPARATE

GO THROUGH

3. Now weave the next strip by separating it and slipping it over the first stationary strip, then through the next, alternating the pattern.

4. Gradually slide the strips toward the curved ends as you weave. If the last strip is too tight, carefully extend the cut slits on the pieces for more room. When the last strip is in place, adjust the strips so they are tight and the weaving forms a nice square of interlocked strips.

ADJUST THE STRIPS AS NEEDED

5. Place some glue between the fabric where the heart shape comes together in the center. Slip one end of the ribbon between and hold until dry. Decide how long you want your handle and glue the other end on the opposite side of the heart in the same way. Then enjoy your heart on your tree or give it a variety of uses! See page 51 for some tiny toys you can make to put inside.

Teeny-Tiny Shopping Bag
(with Teeny-Tiny Gifts!)

Make this little shopping bag from holiday gift wrap and fill it with miniature gifts, each wrapped in festive tissue paper and tied with curled ribbon. Or, fill it with tiny pinecones or greens from the tree, or red and white peppermints or miniature candy canes, and top with a miniature bow.

❄ Materials ❄

Template supplies: tracing paper, craft
    scissors, cereal-box cardboard
Decorative holiday or foil paper, at least
    5" x 7" (12.5 x 17.5 cm)*
Popsicle stick, for creasing folds
Craft glue
Small nail or large needle
Narrow elastic thread or ribbon, 8" (20 cm),
    for hanging

* To make your bag shiny or decorated inside and out, use a 7" x 9" (17.5 x 22.5 cm) sheet of paper and double it over before cutting out the pattern.

To make the bag

1. Trace the SHOPPING BAG template (page 62) onto the tracing paper, marking all score lines. Cut it out. Trace the template, transfer all markings, label, and cut out.

Quick Starts Tips!™

Scoring — not a goal, but scoring paper to get a smooth fold. Simply press a Popsicle stick along the edge of a ruler to "score" an indent in the paper.

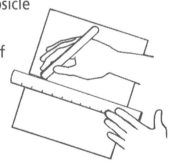

2. Trace the pattern onto the decorative paper. Transfer all markings and cut it out. Score (page 50) all score lines. Fold all scored lines.

3. Fold the bag as shown and glue the tab. Let dry.

4. Fold in the short bottom flaps and fold the longer flaps over them. Glue the last flap in place to form the bottom of the bag.

5. Fold the narrow top edge to the inside of the bag. Glue it in place if you like.

6. With the nail or needle, poke a hole through both top edges for the thread or ribbon to pass through. Thread the elastic or ribbon from the outside to the inside of your bag. Knot the ends on the inside.

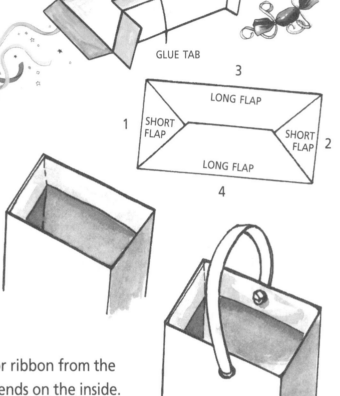

GLUE TAB

3
LONG FLAP
1 SHORT FLAP
SHORT FLAP 2
LONG FLAP
4

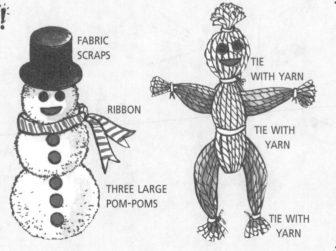

More Quick Starts Fun!

Let me present ... To make a gift-filled ornament, fill the bag half full with batting. Make a pom-pom snowman or yarn doll to peek over the top. Or, wrap three small gifts (small beads, plastic checkers, or mini-erasers) in Christmas paper. Tie the ends with raffia or curling ribbon. Arrange the presents on top so the bag overflows!

FABRIC SCRAPS

RIBBON

THREE LARGE POM-POMS

TIE WITH YARN

TIE WITH YARN

TIE WITH YARN

Shimmering Garland

Move over, popcorn and cranberries! This intricate-looking shiny garland takes the craft of holiday garlands up to a whole new level! The entire garland is actually made out of *paper* — paper beads, that is. The larger interlocking beads are made without any glue, using *origami,* the traditional Japanese art of paper-folding. The smaller *spacers* (narrow beads to string between larger beads) are super-simple to make (you can create a pile of them in no time), and with foil paper they give a truly spectacular effect, shimmering in the lights from your tree! Choose colors that reflect your holiday spirit, and mix and match beads to create the design you want. Then, deck the tree, the hall, and the doorway in festive garlands!

❄ Materials ❄

To make one interlocking origami bead
Card stock, origami, decorative, or metallic
    paper: two 2¾" (7 cm) squares of
    contrasting colors per bead
Popsicle stick, for creasing folds
Pencil

To make interlocking origami beads

1. In this step, it's important to always fold the right sides of the paper together. If you're working with paper that's the same color on both sides, choose one to be the "right" side.

   Fold a square diagonally; open the fold. Fold diagonally the other way; open the fold. Fold in half; open the fold. Fold in half the other way; open the fold. Your paper will look like this.

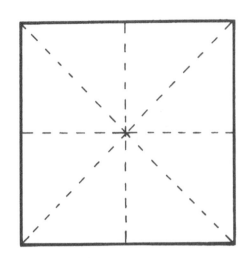

2. Flip the paper over and push down on the center point. Bring two opposite diagonal fold lines together in the center as shown. Fold the flat sides together as shown so that the paper forms a small square.

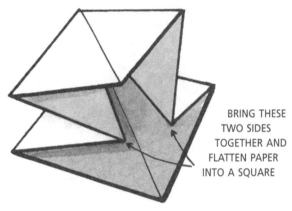

BRING THESE TWO SIDES TOGETHER AND FLATTEN PAPER INTO A SQUARE

CREASE ALL THE EDGES SO THAT IT'S REALLY FLAT

3. Place the square with the folded top pointing up. Fold the triangle section so it is pointing out as shown below.

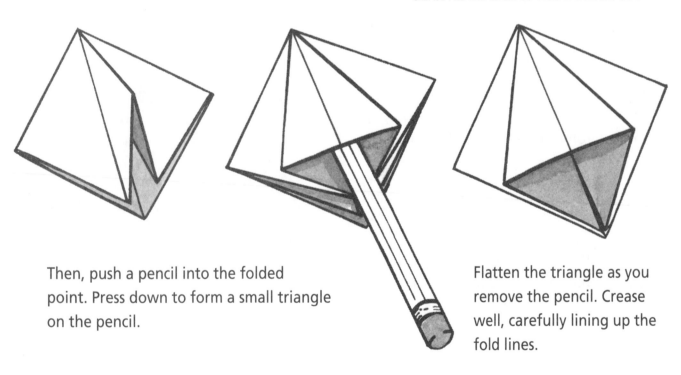

Then, push a pencil into the folded point. Press down to form a small triangle on the pencil.

Flatten the triangle as you remove the pencil. Crease well, carefully lining up the fold lines.

4. Fold the left side of the small triangle over onto the right side and press flat.

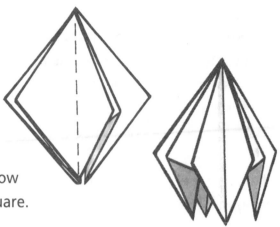

5. Repeat steps 3 and 4 on each of the other three large triangle folds.

   Crease all the fold lines firmly. Congratulations! You've completely folded one half of the bead. Now repeat steps 1 through 5 with the other paper square.

6. Sliding the bead halves together is a little tricky and takes patience. Place the two halves, A and B, on a flat surface. Slide point A of the left half into fold B of the right half, lining up the center folds. Flip to the next section and slide point B into fold A.

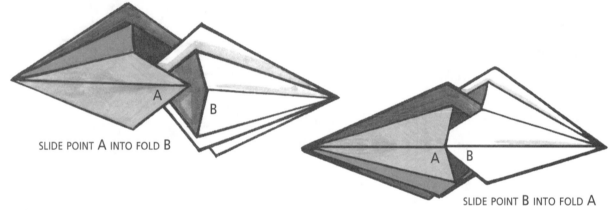

SLIDE POINT A INTO FOLD B

SLIDE POINT B INTO FOLD A

7. Continue working your way around, sliding all the points into the folds.

   You may find that a point has ended up in the wrong fold — just gently pull it out (without pulling out any of the properly positioned points) and slip it into the proper one.

   Take your time, working on one point at a time until you've finished joining the bead halves.

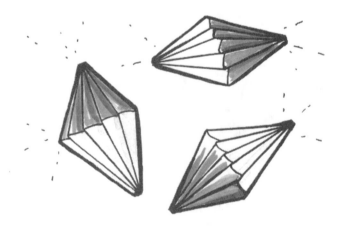

✳ Materials ✳

For the glittery spacer beads
Scissors
Metallic paper
Ruler
Pencil
Toothpick or nail
Glue

To make seven spacer beads

1. Cut a strip of paper about 2" (5 cm) wide and about 6" (15 cm) long. Draw triangles across the strip as shown. Cut the triangles apart.

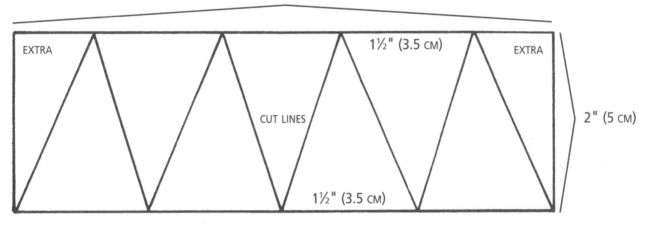

6" (15 CM)

EXTRA

1½" (3.5 CM)

EXTRA

CUT LINES

2" (5 CM)

1½" (3.5 CM)

2. Place the triangle metallic side down. Starting with the wide end, roll it tightly around the toothpick or nail. Glue the end. When you remove the toothpick, it will leave a hole in the middle of the bead. Roll as many beads as you like for using on the garland.

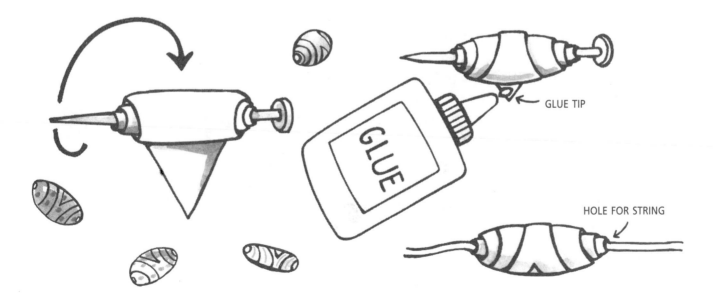

GLUE

GLUE TIP

HOLE FOR STRING

❄ Materials ❄

For the garland

Needle with a large eye or paper clip

Metallic thread or embroidery floss, decorative cord, or yarn

Glue

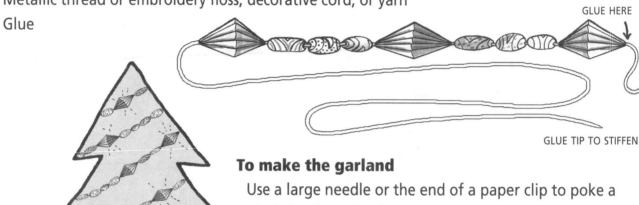

GLUE HERE

GLUE TIP TO STIFFEN

To make the garland

Use a large needle or the end of a paper clip to poke a hole in the ends of each large origami bead. Slip one end of a length of metallic thread or embroidery floss into the hole (apply a little glue to the end of the thread to stiffen it first, if necessary) and add a bit of glue to the end of the bead to hold it in place. String the rolled paper bead spacers on the gold thread. Glue on the next origami bead. Repeat until the garland is the length you want.

More Quick Starts Fun!

- **To make different-sized beads,** change the size of the triangle base. Try spacers made from ½" x 6" (5 mm x 15 cm) strips.
- **For chunkier beads,** use a thicker nail or a pencil. Smaller beads may slip inside chunkier beads, however, so it's best to stick with one bead size for each necklace.
- **For a looser, "springier" bead,** remove the nail and let the bead expand slightly before gluing.
- **Roll cutout photos** from old magazines or catalogs for colorful beads with intriguing designs. When the bead is rolled, you won't see the individual pictures, just the colors.

TEMPLATES

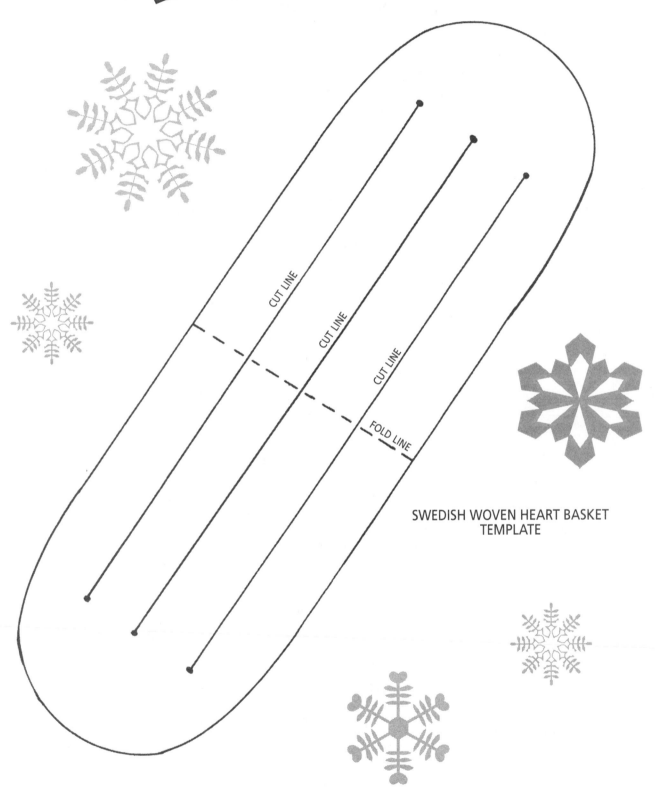

CUT LINE

CUT LINE

CUT LINE

FOLD LINE

SWEDISH WOVEN HEART BASKET
TEMPLATE

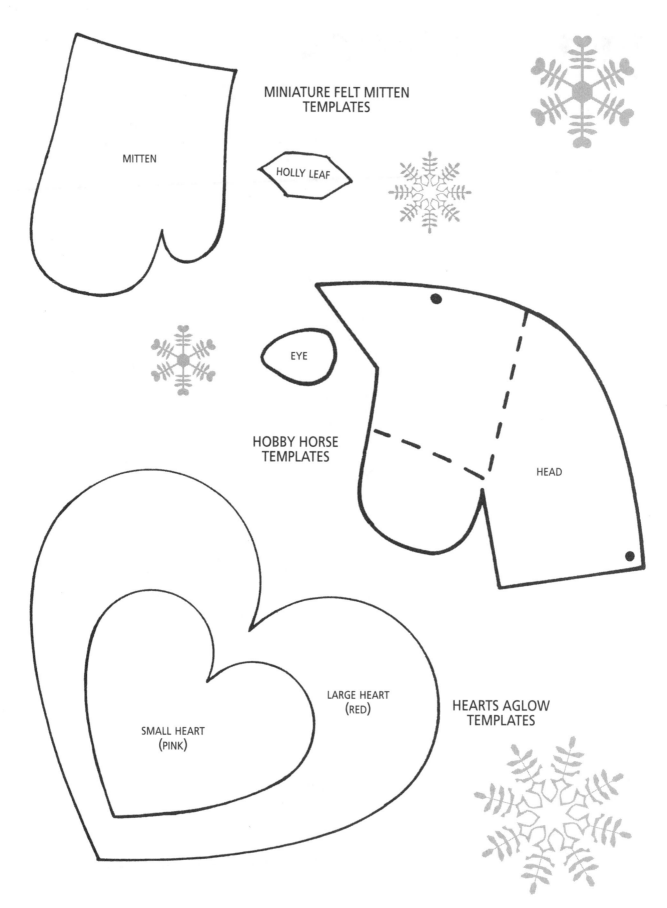

MINIATURE FELT MITTEN
TEMPLATES

MITTEN

HOLLY LEAF

EYE

HOBBY HORSE
TEMPLATES

HEAD

SMALL HEART
(PINK)

LARGE HEART
(RED)

HEARTS AGLOW
TEMPLATES

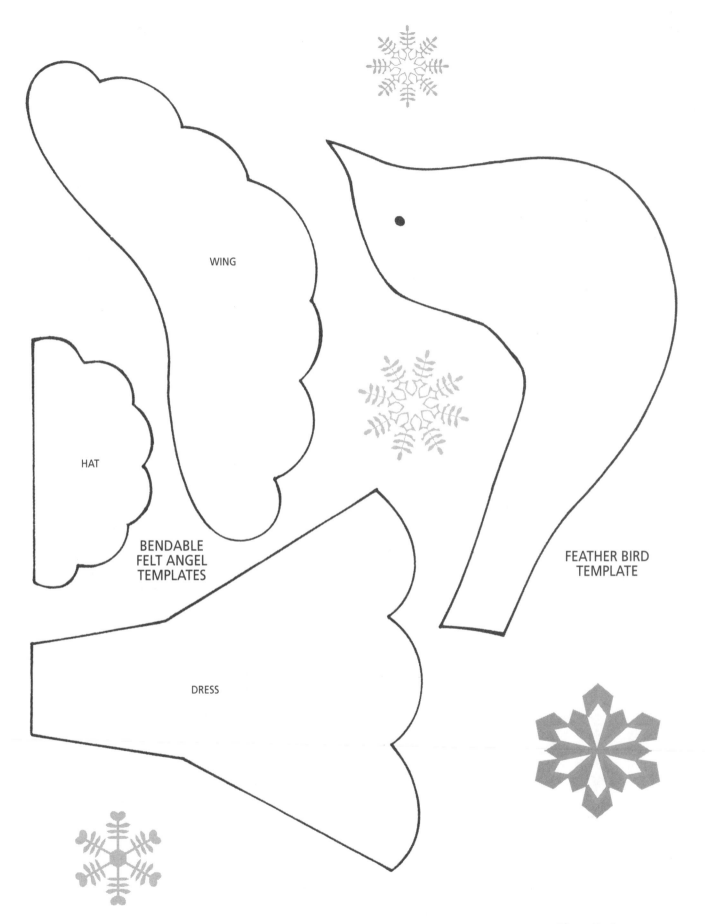

WING

HAT

BENDABLE
FELT ANGEL
TEMPLATES

DRESS

FEATHER BIRD
TEMPLATE

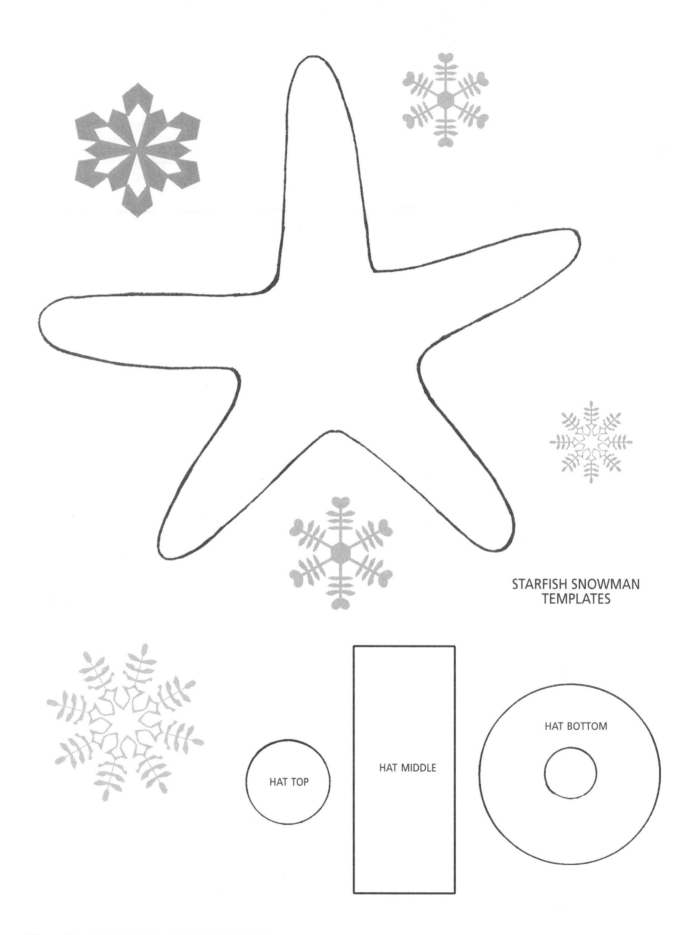

STARFISH SNOWMAN
TEMPLATES

HAT TOP

HAT MIDDLE

HAT BOTTOM

STUFFED TEDDY BEAR
TEMPLATE

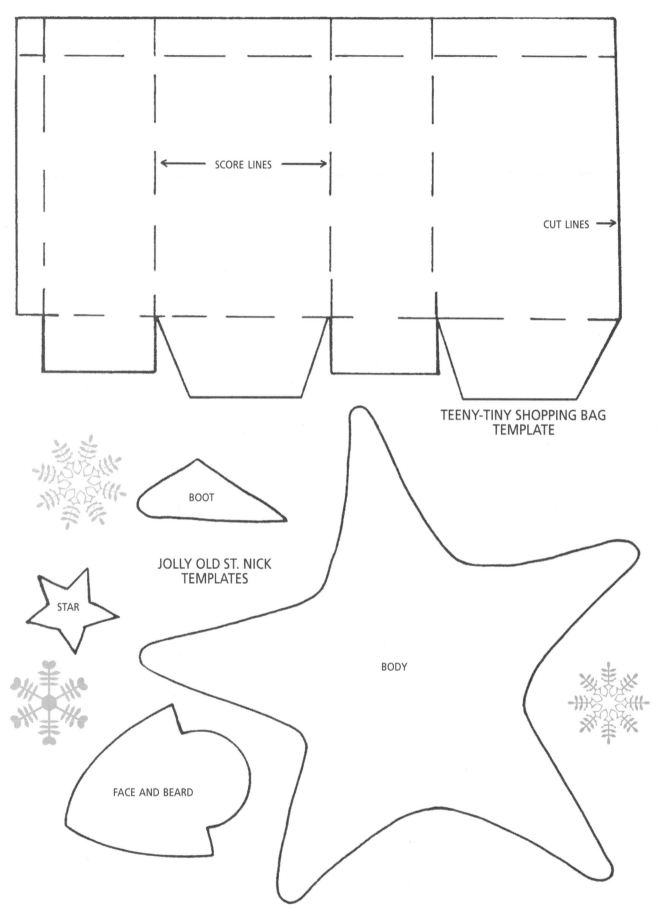

SCORE LINES

CUT LINES

TEENY-TINY SHOPPING BAG
TEMPLATE

BOOT

JOLLY OLD ST. NICK
TEMPLATES

STAR

BODY

FACE AND BEARD

INDEX